ROSA PARKS

*The Courage to
Make a Difference*

AMERICAN HEROES

ROSA PARKS

*The Courage to
Make a Difference*

SNEED B. COLLARD III

Marshall Cavendish
Benchmark
New York

For Karen Gonzales,
my favorite liberty-loving librarian

Marshall Cavendish Benchmark
99 White Plains Road
Tarrytown, New York 10591-9001
www.marshallcavendish.us

Library of Congress Cataloging-in-Publication Data
Collard, Sneed B.
Rosa Parks : the courage to make a difference / by Sneed B. Collard III.
p. cm. — (American heroes)
Summary: "A juvenile biography of Rosa Parks, civil rights activist"—Provided by publisher.
Includes bibliographical references and index.
ISBN-13: 978-0-7614-2163-4
ISBN-10: 0-7614-2163-7
1. Parks, Rosa, 1913–2005—Juvenile literature. 2. African American women—Alabama—Montgomery—Biography—
Juvenile literature. 3. African Americans—Alabama—Montgomery—Biography—Juvenile literature. 4. Civil rights
workers—Alabama—Montgomery—Biography—Juvenile literature. 5. African Americans—Civil rights—Alabama—
Montgomery—History—20th century—Juvenile literature. 6. Segregation in transportation—Alabama—
Montgomery—History—20th century—Juvenile literature. 7. Montgomery (Ala.)—Race relations—Juvenile literature.
8. Montgomery (Ala.)—Biography—Juvenile literature. I. Title. II. Series: Collard, Sneed B. American heroes.
F334.M753C65 2006
323.092—dc22   [B]   2006012996

Editor: Joyce Stanton
Editorial Director: Michelle Bisson
Art Director: Anahid Hamparian
Series Designer and Compositor: Anne Scatto / PIXEL PRESS
Printed in Malaysia
1 3 5 6 4 2

Images provided by Rose Corbett Gordon, Art Editor,
Mystic, CT, from the following sources:
Front cover: From AMERICANS WHO TELL THE
TRUTH by Robert Shetterly, copyright by Robert
Shetterly. Used by permission of Dutton Children's
Books, A Division of Penguin Young Readers Group,
A Member of Penguin Group (USA) Inc., 345 Hudson
Street, New York, NY 10014. All rights reserved.
Back cover: Hulton Archive/Getty Images.

Pages i, 8, 15, 16, 24, 34: Bettmann/Corbis;
page ii: Trinity Wholesale; *page vi, 19:* Time & Life
Pictures/Getty Images; *pages vii, 3, 11:* Library
of Congress; *page 4:* Hulton Archive/Getty Images;
pages 7, 12, 23, 27: Time Life Pictures/Getty Images;
page 20: The Granger Collection, NY;
page 28: Flip Schulke/Corbis; *page 31:* Rebecca
Cook/Reuters/Corbis; *page 32:* Getty Images.

Contents

Rosa Parks stayed in her seat on a bus. Her simple act changed the world.

Rosa Parks

Sometimes a single action can change the world. It doesn't have to be grand or showy. It can be simple, like staying in your seat. That's what Rosa Parks did more than fifty years ago. Since then, the world has never been the same.

Rosa was born on February 4, 1913, in Tuskegee, Alabama. Her parents named her Rosa Louise McCauley. Her mother, Leona, was a schoolteacher. Her father, James McCauley, worked as a carpenter. But, when Rosa was only two and a half years old, her father left the family to find work. Rosa would rarely see him after that. Instead, she was raised by her mother and grandparents in the tiny town of Pine Level, Alabama.

Rosa grew up in a tiny Alabama town where most people knew each other.

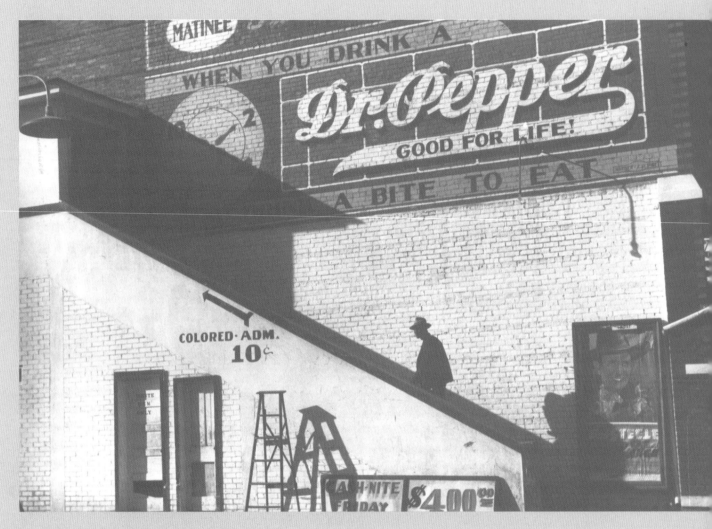

When Rosa was a girl, black people in the South had to use separate entrances and sit in separate sections of movie theaters.

In Pine Level, Rosa's mother and grandparents taught her many things. One of these things was to respect herself. Rosa's grandfather had been born a slave. He had been treated very badly and didn't want his family to suffer as he had.

Unfortunately, when Rosa was a little girl, she and other black Americans still were treated unfairly. Laws in the South kept them apart from whites.

Fifty years earlier, the Civil War had ended slavery. But in many places in the South, black people did not have the basic rights that white people enjoyed. They could not vote. They could not live where they wanted. They could not use the same public facilities that white people used. Black people who tried to stand up for their rights were often jailed or killed by whites. Rosa's grandparents and mother taught Rosa that this was wrong.

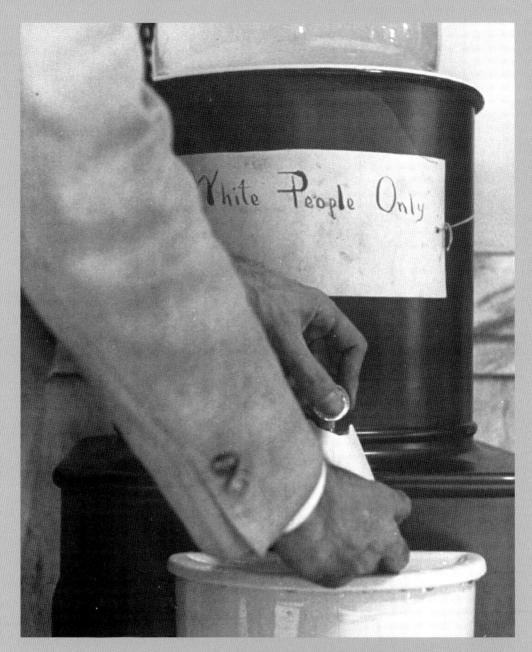

Only white people could use this water cooler.

*Classrooms for black children were often
crowded, dark, and dreary.*

Many black people tried to improve their lives by getting an education. This wasn't easy. Schools for white children usually had plenty of teachers and supplies. Schools for black children did not. Some didn't even have windows or desks. In Rosa's elementary school, fifty to sixty children from grades one through six all squeezed into a single classroom.

Rosa had to leave school in the eleventh grade. Both her grandmother and mother were ill. Rosa had to take care of them. "I was not happy about dropping out of school," she later wrote. "It was just something that had to be done."

Soon, though, Rosa met someone who would change her life. His name was Raymond Parks. Rosa married Raymond in 1932, when she was nineteen years old. Raymond was a barber. He also was an *activist*—someone who works hard to improve life for others. He helped raise money for blacks who had been unfairly arrested for crimes. Later he worked registering black people to vote.

Raymond's barber shop probably looked much like this one.
It was for black people only.

*Members of the Ku Klux Klan hide behind masks and long white
robes during one of their frightening ceremonies. The KKK was a secret society
of white people who tried to prevent black people from gaining their rights.*

In the 1930s, black Americans did not have the same voting rights as white Americans. Many states had laws that made it almost impossible for blacks to vote. As a result, black people had little to say about what laws were made or how their country was governed.

By the 1940s, many activists, both black and white, began working to change the voting laws. This work was dangerous. Police often arrested or beat up the activists. A group called the Ku Klux Klan, or KKK, bombed their houses. Sometimes activists were even shot or hanged.

Rosa admired the work that the activists did. Soon she also worked on projects to help her people. One project would make Rosa famous. It was the desegregation of public buses.

For years, southern states had practiced *segregation*. This was the policy of keeping white people and black people apart. Blacks had to use different water fountains than white people. They had to sleep in different hotels and eat at different restaurants. They even had to sit in different sections of public buses.

Throughout the South, unfair laws kept
black people apart from whites.

Rosa was a quiet person. Who would have thought that she would turn the law upside down!

Black people especially hated the busing laws. In Montgomery, Alabama, the city where Rosa and Raymond lived, blacks and whites had to sit in separate rows on the buses. Only white people could sit in the front rows. Black people could sit in the middle, but if the front rows were full, they had to move to the back to let a white person sit down. To change this unfair system, black leaders needed someone to challenge the law.

Rose never imagined she would be that person!

On December 1, 1955, Rosa boarded a bus to ride home from work. She took an empty seat in the middle near some other black passengers. At another stop, several white people boarded. They filled all of the empty "white seats" in the front, but one white man was left standing. The bus driver looked at Rosa and the other black riders. "Let me have those seats," he told them.

The black people sitting next to Rosa moved to the rear of the bus. Rosa didn't. She wasn't trying to be a hero. She wasn't tired, either. She was just tired of being treated differently because of the color of her skin.

When Rosa boarded the bus on December 1, 1955,
she had no idea she would be making history.

Rosa was arrested and fingerprinted after she refused to move to the back of the bus.

The police came and arrested Rosa. They took her to jail. A few days later, the court found her guilty of breaking the city's busing laws. But local black leaders decided to use Rosa's arrest to challenge Montgomery's busing laws. They formed a new group called the Montgomery Improvement Association. They put a young minister named Dr. Martin Luther King Jr. in charge.

The Montgomery Improvement Association demanded that the city change the busing laws. The city refused. So Dr. King and other leaders organized a boycott of Montgomery's buses. For the next year, blacks stayed off the buses. The boycott hurt the bus company and local businesses. Police harassed those who wouldn't ride the bus, but no one gave an inch.

For a year, black citizens of Montgomery, Alabama, stayed off the city's buses. They did a lot of walking!

Dr. King refused to end the boycott,
even after his own house was bombed.

The boycott made many white people extremely angry. Dr. King's home was bombed. Some whites even telephoned Rosa and threatened to kill her for what she was doing. "It was frightening to get those calls," Rosa remembered. She could have backed out of the fight against the busing laws, but she didn't. She believed in fair treatment for all people—even though it meant putting her life in danger.

Rosa flew all over the country to speak about the busing laws and other civil rights issues. In February 1956, a black lawyer named Fred Gray filed a lawsuit in federal court on behalf of Rosa and four other women. The lawsuit claimed that bus segregation was unfair and illegal. On November 13, 1956, the United States Supreme Court agreed. This decision ended the busing laws.

Rosa was glad to board a bus after winning the lawsuit.
Now she could sit wherever she liked.

In 1966, for the first time in the state of Alabama, whites and blacks waited in line together to vote.

Rosa witnessed many more successes in the fight for civil rights. The greatest came in 1964, when President Lyndon Johnson signed the Civil Rights Act. This new set of laws guaranteed blacks the right to vote. It allowed people of all races to use all public facilities anywhere. It also said that anyone who broke these new laws would be punished. The Civil Rights Act ended segregation in the United States.

Even after the Civil Rights Act, Rosa kept working to improve the lives of black Americans. In the 1980s, she was honored for her role in the fight for civil rights. Streets were named after her. The Smithsonian Institution put up a bronze statue of her. On December 1, 2000—forty-five years exactly after Rosa's arrest—Troy University in Montgomery, Alabama, opened the Rosa L. Parks Library and Museum in her honor.

Rosa became so famous that, in towns and cities across America,
streets were named after her.

Rosa's simple act helped make the world a better place for all of us.

Rosa Parks died on October 24, 2005. All over the world, people gathered to remember her. She was a person who stood up for what she believed. Her life will always remind us that taking even simple steps can make the world a better place forever.

IMPORTANT DATES

1913 Born on February 4 in Tuskegee, Alabama.

1918 Begins school in Pine Level, Alabama.

1929 Leaves school to take care of her mother and grandmother.

1932 Marries Raymond Parks.

1933 Receives her high school diploma after going back to school.

1943 Becomes secretary for the local chapter of the NAACP (National Association for the Advancement of Colored People).

1955 Arrested for and found guilty of not giving up her seat to a white man on a Montgomery bus; boycott of buses begins.

1956 United States Supreme Court declares that segregation on buses is illegal.

1957 Moves to Detroit with her husband.

1963 Attends the Civil Rights March on Washington in Washington, DC.

1964 President Johnson signs the Civil Rights Act.

1977 Husband, Raymond, dies.

1987 Co-founds the Rosa and Raymond Parks Institute for Self-Development.

2000 The Rosa L. Parks Library and Museum dedicated at Troy University in Montgomery, Alabama.

2005 Dies on October 24 in Detroit, Michigan.

WORDS TO KNOW

activist A person who works to support a project that he or she believes is just and fair.

boycott To refuse (usually with other people) to deal with a person or an organization; a boycott is usually done to protest something that is unfair.

civil rights The rights of every citizen of a country. In the United States, a citizen's civil rights include the right to speak freely, the right to vote, the right to live anywhere, and the right to equal protection under the law.

desegregate To stop the practice of keeping people of different races apart.

federal court A court or group of judges that represents the entire nation.

harass To repeatedly bother or threaten someone.

register To officially sign up in order to do something, such as vote.

segregation The policy of keeping white people and black people apart.

slavery The practice of owning other human beings.

South The southern part of the United States.

To Learn More about Rosa Parks

WEB SITES

Academy of Achievement: Rosa Parks
 www.achievement.org/autodoc/page/par0pro-1
The Courage of Rosa Parks
 www.nationalgeographic.com/ngkids/9802/rosaparks
The Rosa Parks Bus at Henry Ford Museum
 www.hfmgv.org/exhibits/rosaparks
Rosa Parks Library and Museum
 http://montgomery.troy.edu/museum

BOOKS

If a Bus Could Talk: The Story of Rosa Parks by Faith Ringgold. Simon & Schuster, 1999.

A Picture Book of Rosa Parks by David A. Adler. Holiday House, 1993.

Rosa Parks: Civil Rights Pioneer by Erika L. Shores. Capstone Press, 2005.

Rosa Parks: Meet a Civil Rights Hero by Edith Hope Fine. Enslow
Publishers, 2004.

Rosa Parks: My Story by Rosa Parks. Puffin Books, 1999.

PLACES TO VISIT

Martin Luther King, Jr., National Historic Site
450 Auburn Avenue, NE
Atlanta, Georgia 30312-1525
PHONE: (404) 331-5190 WEB SITE: **http://www.nps.gov/malu/**

Rosa Parks Library and Museum
252 Montgomery Street
Montgomery, Alabama 36104
PHONE: (334) 241-8661 WEB SITE:
http://montgomery.troy.edu/museum/

Smithsonian Anacostia Museum & Center for African American
History and Culture
1901 Fort Place, SE
Washington, DC 20020
PHONE: (202) 633-4820 WEB SITE: **http://anacostia.si.edu/**

Smithsonian National Museum of American History
14th Street and Constitution Avenue, NW
Washington, DC 20560
PHONE: (202) 633-1000 WEB SITE: **http://americanhistory.si.edu**

INDEX

Page numbers for illustrations are in boldface.

ABOUT THE AUTHOR

SNEED B. COLLARD III is the author of more than fifty award-winning books for young people, including *The Prairie Builders*; *A Platypus, Probably*; *One Night in the Coral Sea*; and the four-book SCIENCE ADVENTURES series for Marshall Cavendish Benchmark. In addition to his writing, Sneed is a popular speaker and presents widely to students, teachers, and the general public. In 2006, he was selected as the Washington Post–Children's Book Guild Nonfiction Award winner for his achievements in children's writing. He is also the author of several novels for young adults, including *Dog Sense* and *Flash Point*. To learn more about Sneed, visit his Web site at www.sneedbcollardiii.com.